MEMOIR OF
A GHOST

MEMOIR OF
A GHOST

KALA CULLARS

Kala Cullars

Table of Contents

The Making of Alaksraluk.. 4

Origin-The Cuckoo's Nest. 5

Beliefs. 8

Child Puppy. 11

An Abandoned Womb. 13

July 6, 2015 - 15

Drunken Jargon. 15

A Cyst of Sisters. 19

Childhood Canker Sores. 20

The Water Forgot Us. 22

Father No1247. 25

Paper People. 26

Perfect Parents. 27

I Kept Dating My Dad. 28

Body Tag. 29

African American Antagonists. 31

Hoarding Ghosts. 32

The New-Age Negro. 33

Courting the Colored. 35

African American Antagonists. 36

Tree-Cat & Mouse. 38

Should Lives Matter?. 39

Born Guilty of Treason. 41

Unrequited American Lover. 43

Being Black in Public. 45

Nesting Dolls. 48

I Am a Woman of Grace and Dignity.. 50

Provoked in Thought. 51

The Hoarder. 53

The Psychic Reader. 54

Unsalable. 55

Telekinesis. 57

Trauma. 58

The Myth of Madness. 60

Anxiety. 63

Know-It-All 66

Crazy Glue. 68

I Worked at a Car. 69

Dealership. 69

Poetry Submission. 72

The Writer. 75

Pockets. 77

I Must Be Rid. 79

Social MEDIA-crity. 81

Woman. 82

The Rebellion.. 83

Transactional Worshipper. 83

Identity Crisis. 85

The Pariah & the Piranha. 88

Feline Frequency. 90

Self-Departed. 92

Lost My Voice Again. 96

Relapse. 97

51st Street. 99

They Told Me You Weren't Dead. 100

A dormant Depression. 102

Rendezvous with a Mute Narcissist. 103

Cracks in the Marble. 105

Layaway Lovers. 107

The Actress. 109

The Making of Alaksraluk

Origin-The Cuckoo's Nest

8052 S. Escanaba:
wings clipped,
the wind a tease
beneath a broken spirit.
A sanctuary for insanity,
a safe haven for the wicked.
My dilapidated home,
the squalid structure
ominously hoarding the hoarder,
muddled by mediocrity.
Landfill
of paternally mutilated
umbilical cords.
Filth-fed and bred to fail
African American nuclear family,
an *a priori* truth,
the pungency of poverty.
I was born and raised
on the South Side of Chicago

in an impoverished neighborhood
littered with abandonment—
foreclosed properties,
vacant dreams,
and children left behind.
A cesspool
for criminality that manufactured
society's delinquents.
It was home
to America's most unwanted.
It was a neighborhood
pigmented with dark pain
overpopulated with the purged.
Mutated offspring.
During my teenage years
my posture still remained
as unformed as the spinal
cord of an infant.
My mother's womb is the cause
and I the defect.
Choke collar fastened
to a retractable umbilical cord,
violently reeling
me back to the heels
of the oppressor.
Knees pulled inward,
fractured in the fetal position,
internally cracked from
the sheer volume of my rebellious cries.
Held in the grip of maternal misery,

although she has not the slightest grip
on reality.

I am forgiving that which has happened in the past.
I am choosing to heal.
I am rewriting old memories according to ideals.
I am choosing to love.
I am sending love to my mother's inner child.
I am choosing to feel.

Beliefs

meet needs at the time
from parents' parents and so on
like a subscription renewing,
a vicarious ensuing.
Umbilical cord elongated,
birth prolonged.
Biased,
belligerent,
belittling.
You're just like your ol' rotten, no good daddy, she believed.
Soon enough, I did too.
Egotistical,
limiting,
lifelong.
You're too fat. No one is going to want you.
Indifferently echoed and force-fed
seedless beliefs.
This is a house of God, not gay.
Insidiously inherited ideas,
bed made inside your mind.
Rest your head on the repeated rendition

of reality recited as you were reared.
And I was tucked in again.
Breech thought:
Who will stop the bleed?
Heal the mental wound,
prune the weeds?
To whom do you belong?
Inseminated indiscriminately
and off you sprung.
If found, return to owner.
Reward: sanity.
Product of experience, environment, and ignorance.
Unthink, unlearn, question.
Then discern, learn to think.
Learn to learn.

I accept myself as I am.
I am renewed in how I believe and behave.
I am choosing to align with my destination,
rather than to reflect on my origin.
I am gracefully putting one foot in front of the other.
I am forgiving the trespasses of others
as I would like to be forgiven.
I am purposefully thinking positive thoughts

Child Puppy

I wanted to go too.
I wanted to be a part of
the action, the movement, people
going somewhere, doing something,
becoming someone.
I wanted to hang out with the big kids,
with my older cousins.
I wanted to be liked,
I wanted to be accepted, I wanted to be in a gang.
I was always the follower.
I never had a mind of my own
is what my mother would tell me.
I followed myself into adulthood
Perusing for more reasons to hate myself
on Instagram. I want to go too.
I want to be successful.
I want to be liked.
I want to be followed.
I want to be accepted. I want to be in a cult.
I want a mentor. I want a new leader.
I want to be led gently toward anywhere

that isn't the dead end that my parents were.
I want to love. I want to accept myself.
I want that for others too.
I want to be a leader.
I want to lead others
back to the truth of who they are.
I have to first find the way myself.

I am following the lead of a Higher Power.
I am leading by example.
I am led inward.
I am unapologetically who I am.

An Abandoned Womb

Hardened ovarian cysts.
Unborn childbearing the cross
of its parents' shit
smeared like blessed oil on the fingertips,
forming makeshift crosses,
faith greased onto the back door.
Black homes don't need gargoyles.
Breathing hard, tissue scarred, hands in fists.
Half past an abortion and slit wrists.
I always wanted you, my mother tells me. Fetus convulsing
from the sound of an outward hell, boisterous blows
of a man in a mental cell.
Faint beat pulsating irregularly to a beating.
Father imposed on a beat down mother,
brutalizing both egg and shell.
A baby beaten on its forehead,
third eye fortified with callouses and fractures.
Heavy in your womb, heavy in your scorn.
Too heavy for your arms.
Nursing a daughter who's
already estranged in a warped cocoon.

I am alive.
I am radiant in my resilience.
I am whole.
I am at home in the world.

July 6, 2015 - Drunken Jargon

Lengths spent in a used uterus,
coaxed from the gutter,
birthed in the sewage of a fallen world.
Grime cements malformed eyelids.
Induction to the grid,
a placenta of ink
in womb and in wound,
in thought and in trauma.
My heart murmurs
in a foreign language.
I was born into a fallen nest.
In reflecting on the allure
of accolades and high-ticket items,
I've come to realize that it's all an illusion.
I recall a time
in which everything I currently have was a want.
I recall a time
in which I didn't even feel worthy
of the desire.

In acquiring
more things,
the craving is only temporarily sated.
Happiness is
relaxing into the now.
Happiness is
in the acquisition itself.
It's in the journey.
The journey is the destination.
Happiness is in gratitude.
While it's not always easy-
being that we live in a material world,
God is the only
real.
need.
and that knowing *is* happiness.
I'm thinking about this moment-
how I'll look back upon it
and regret having looked forward
instead of simply being.
What is with this fixation on the fix
that is the future?
The illusion is
that once I acquire
the dream job, dream car, dream lover,
dream etcetera, then I'll be happy,
as if happiness can't be felt now
in anticipation of the good to come.
It's like
getting your favorite doll for Christmas

but not knowing how to enjoy it
because the novelty is prematurely worn.
I've always needed
both of my marshmallows with immediacy.
Conditioned to need conditions
to love and live.
It's the realization
that other people aren't paying me any mind,
but it's all in my mind
and they're caught up
in their own being,
at home in this world.
Something I've never been.
When I think of concerts and summer festivities,
I think of how watered down my memory is
because until now, I never experienced any of it sober.
I've always been a storyteller.
In my earlier days I learned
that telling stories was used
interchangeably with telling lies.
In therapy someone's primary concern
is to take care of your mind for that hour.
Their goal is to help you get into the solution.
Their job is *you*.
Today I hear myself
On the tongue of the mind
of someone else.
From this day forward
I have decided
to not chase anyone ever again.

I will hold my power.

I will not make anyone more important than me.

If I can only start with holding a train of thought.

I am remembering to breathe.

I am pausing when necessary.

I am grounding myself in the never ending now.

I am choosing to be sober, just for today.

I am counting my blessings.

I am worth listening to.

I deserve to be heard.

I am focused on the good.

A Cyst of Sisters

Directionless.
Stupefied in stagnation.
Broken
internal compass encompasses
a disappointing deity.
Blaming God
To avoid the mirror.
Wade in blood with iron feet.
Shackled in shame
The fool dreams,
DNA incomplete.
I am accountable.
I am proud of who I am.
I am progressing.
I am trusting my intuition.
To regress does not negate my progress.

Childhood Canker Sores

Energy in backward motion.
Shame, shame, shame.
He grabbed me by the collar.
Lyrics to the hand game I played as a schoolgirl,
now a soundtrack to adulthood.
Hidden behind the tonsils of anxiety,
held stationary in the teeth of society.
Violent swing of emotions—
such a nuisance, like one eye swollen shut.
Two hearts in backward,
a mosquito bite beneath the skin.
Childhood house boarded up.
Who I've been is haunting me again.
"I was pregnant with you", my mother said.
"While you were in utero
Someone else asked to share my womb.
I birthed you both together
beneath two moons
so you'd never be on your own, nor your own."
I am healing the timeline.
I am allowed to be someone other than who I've been.

I am allowed to change.
I am allowed to grow.

The Water Forgot Us

In conversations I don't speak
of my upbringing.
Drains begrudgingly coughed up water.
With a tired arm extended, I'd fill up empty jugs,
careful not to let the emptiness fill me,
saving the water for the financial forecast:
precipitated poverty.
It's not that I've forgotten playing Russian roulette
with the shower or faucet,
praying to the world of my mind
that my grandfather had dug up the lawn
to find the magical pipe and rigged it again,
or the days in which the water cut off
mid-shower and the soap cast me into a waxen figure.
when shampoo was still nestled on my eyelids,
so I stared at the toilet bowl in deep contemplation
wondering which would yield the worst infection:
dirty water, or soap left in places where it shouldn't be?
Or yelling at my younger cousin
through the paper-thin floor,
I need to use the water.

For water couldn't flow
to both apartments at the same time.
So, the water she gave me.
The people at the water company were marathoners,
and we'd never catch up to them.
Or how the pilot on the furnace had to be lit
by my crackhead uncle,
and how the smell of gasoline was welcomed,
for soon the wintry draft would meet its match.
How it wailed beneath the plastic
duct-taped to the windows.
I don't speak about tiptoeing
in my house slippers around
the trail of blood that stained the back porch steps
shed from pit bulls pitted against one another,
mirroring the crazed angst of the black men
who owned them and yet were still owned themselves.
Or how my heart broke
because there was room in my arms for those dogs.
I'd chide against my grandfather and cousins,
You are but monsters among men,
and they'd laugh at my 9-year-old threats
to call Animal Cruelty.
And sometimes I'd actually call,
and then hang up because it meant
that it would be the last I'd see of those dogs.
I wouldn't be able to sneak them water
in their dirt-covered bowls
or try to communicate with them telepathically.
The dogs, like me, made of mostly water,

but still dehydrated—wading in the shallow,
broken paradigm of my kin.
Stay away from that dog. He's a fight dog,
my cousin would yell.
Dogs that were as untrusting of the world as I was.
We understood one another.
I am honoring other people as they are.
I am allowing God to be God in infinite manifestations—
all here with a cause and a course.
I am hydrated.
I am flooded with abundance.
I have been monster and man. Therefore, how am I to condemn?
I am releasing the inclination to be judge and jury.
I am replacing this with acceptance for those
with different struggles.
I am showered in abundance.
I am rinsed of all judgment

Father No1247

The iciness of iron bars
deadens the nerves in his palm's dim lifeline.
Each fragment of the sentence speaks:
Father, please be forgiven
for you knew not who you are:
still my shining star.
Palpitating to no rhythm in particular,
a paper paradise of letters
is where we can exist together
outside of the system, perpendicular.
When you live fast like we did
you're either dead or always at a dead end,
resurrecting ourselves with uppers so the night won't end.
As free as the mind, as free as the human.
I am mentally free.
I am liberated in the renewal
of my spirit and spine.
I am spiritually and emotionally liberated.

Paper People

Paper cut, paper womb,
confetti afterbirth, after-party,
paper pain, paper people,
paupers eating paper food,
paper chain gang,
run-of-the-mill paper,
ruled paper, decreased margins,
painting your portrait
over the obituaries
in the Chicago Tribune Newspaper.
I am redefining my margins.
I am coloring outside of the lines.
I am aligned.

Perfect Parents

Pointed fingers at imperfect parents
picked up the bruised fallen apple
from the dying tree.
Walking through life,
eyes watering with wanting
a wing that would shelter
a mere feather,
anything better
failing to realize that
I chose two parents
who were also God in disguise.
whose inner divinity
could only be realized
through forgiving eyes

I am the daughter of Divine Mother.
I am the daughter of the Heavenly Father.
I am a child of the Universe.
I am an extension of Source Energy.

I Kept Dating My Dad

to reveal
what still
needed to heal.

Why do you keep letting him come back? I'd ask
Because
I don't want you to grow up without a dad,
my mom would say.
Dormant autoimmune disease.
As I got older, my dad began
to return in non-physical manners an
affectionate affliction for the avoidant type
reenacting the same grim grime and gripe or
dating the ones that were high as a kite
strung out, picking a fight while in flight
I am accepting my parents for who they are.
I am releasing judgment of their best.
I am sending love to both
my mother and father's inner children.

Body Tag

I hoard
people and emotions,
a conditioned response to deprivation.
What's far more frightening
is that I hoard the emotions of others as well,
People of other people
die vicariously through some,
and are birthed deeper into existence by most.
I'm always habitually sampling the tastes of others,
savoring each flavor of their truth.
A virgin identity is an impossibility.
I synchronize this plethora of individuals,
creating the soundtrack of the varied lives I've lived,
overlapped with the lives of those t
hat have lived within me.
Halves of wholes.
Spirits in subliminal memories.
During my early twenties I lacked self-awareness,
obedient to the patterns sewn in my fingers,
a malnourished identity craving a safe place to feed.
Bed sores plague every inch of my sense of self,

determinedly writhing in excrement,
praying into stale air for a transfiguration of some sort,
hands torn from palm to forefinger
from foolishly trying to hold on to past agonies.
Lines of my life expelled to heal chafed lifelines.
The familiarity of the sorrow was maliciously comforting.
Grief cradled me unconditionally.
Quite contrarily, happiness was a stranger
of whom I feared rejection,
still afraid to touch the truth.
The former in its entirety is honest, yet safe.
I am content with who I am.
I am self-satisfied.
I am reveling in release and relief.
I am increasingly self-aware.
I am honoring all parts of my journey.
I am emotionally intelligent.

African American
Antagonists

Hoarding Ghosts

Deformity of faith.
Organs inflamed and dreams in the fire.
The formidable rat race.
Inorganic perspiration.
This night, this anemic fire.
This dirty desire.
Sleeping in stables.
Sheep eating at my table.
Watch me dance
while tethered in your fable—
a blank, nomadic soul.
I am roaring with resilience.
I am undefeated.

The New-Age Negro

Cabrini Green, the new guillotine.
Electric slide into the electric chair.
Headless slaves chained in Plato's cave.
Shadows distract them from the sight of their graves.
Spine growing concave, a grave sight to see.
Sleight of hand helping the economy,
hand-me-down pity is their embellishment.
Astonishment at the alleged abolishment.
Still not free, still displaced, still the wrong race.
Why still the long face?
As if I can't still taste the fecal waste
on my black ancestor's face.
Eyes that erratically emulate empathy,
walks like an enemy, talks with no affinity for me.
I say this candidly:
That nigga ain't no kin to me.
Black prisoners locked away in Azkaban,
got the Taliban policing the South Side
like it's Afghanistan.
The news a nuisance
and a New Age noose nonsense.

I am allowed to transcend ancestral pain.
I am practicing forgiveness for my mental well being.
I am allowed to forgive and not condone.
I need neither restitution or retribution
to arrive at an internal resolution.

Courting the Colored

Oh, Lordy, pick a bailiff.
Good riddance written in blood.
The prosecutor that'll prostitute her or him,
perjure her own kin.
Protect the color of her own sin,
protect the judicial skin, project her own spin.
A pigment not meant to win
unless it's O.J. Simpson.
Day, me say day-o, jay, jail-o.
Sentenced to life in prison
and me wanna go home.
6 foot 7 foot 8 foot down,
brown wooden box,
brown skin in the ground.
I am a law-abiding citizen.
I am freed by the fruits of my faith.
I am faithful.
I am praying to the most Supreme.

African American Antagonists

Spoken from a forked tongue
perched behind pursed lips of privilege:
I hope you fare well on welfare,
mental medication, mediocrity, and Medicare.
My hooded silhouette a scare
breathing borrowed air,
bullet burrowed into his back.
Loaded with skin-earned animosity
Borrowed another life you can't give back.
Whiplash from how quickly a blind eye is turned.
Another black fades to black.
Well, we the people think that's fair.
Skin that's fair, blue-eyed stare.
You create your own reality.
Therefore, you antagonize this brutality
instead of cashing government checks.
Could've took the noose from around your neck
and jumped rope, lassoed hope, got back on the boat.
We didn't deal your demographic dope.

Stay afloat on a landfill surrounded by slippery slopes.
Strange fruits of our labor—
Estranged roots cannot anchor,
homeless on our homeland.
We didn't promise you land,
you're but 3/5ths of a man,
deemed a dividend on demand
at the command of the man.
I am whole.
I am whole.
I am rooted in a greater reason.
I am grounded.
I am strong.
I am unstoppable.

Tree-Cat & Mouse

Tree-cat and mouse,
treehouse and senate.
Sentence the witness
minding his business.
Truth turned indifference.
Neck hangs from the judicial branch,
free trial of democracy.
Trial in a tree, another mock policy.
Dangle the child from an apple tree.
Trauma runs in the family.
I am healing.
I am a role model.
I am a trailblazer for those who will
come after me.
I am an example that change is possible.

Should Lives Matter?

Black lives,
for that matter.
Blasted into black matter.
Ashes scattered.
Black boy's last breath
permeates white
sky, black
lives strung out
to air dry.
Black organs sprinkled like confetti.
Pieces of grandma Betty.
Human piñata swings to moonlight sonata,
rocking steady.
Does only Miranda have rights?
Because she's white?
Brought a bag of candy to a gunfight.
Black lives matter sometimes.
No rhyme or reason, just hunting season.
Be a good sport, support human blood sport.
Swing batter batter, black skin cells splatter
like 400-year-old birthday cake batter.

Brain cells sprinkle, scatter,
cementing the chatter of concrete wrong beliefs
like blacks can't speak.
Kiss my asphalt black, ashen cheeks.
Cut down from the tree in the nick of time,
nicked his spine. Blackened skin, black eyes
peek, black-eyed peas, black fleas, black pleas.
Block all the black out, girl got her back out,
no rhyme or reason. Got her head blown back,
brains out the back beyond a reasonable doubt.
They are alive.
They are human.
Internally, we are the same.
They are us.
Why do we continue to kill ourselves—
conned by the illusion of separateness and superiority?

Born Guilty of Treason

Black lungs,
I can't breathe,
iron grip
power trip.
Emancipation proclamation, anticipation 2050?
Freedom's ringing in deaf ears.
Post-Trump reconstruction.
Philando Castille, steel toe boot
on my throat stagnates the South.
American sandcastles, dreams made of sand.
Sandman is Uncle Sam, Sandra Bland, swollen glands.
Cuckoo's nest without a clue and in a clan,
banding together, clucking in the cuckoo's nest.
Mind span, time span, mind spent,
mind
served.
White
house, white picket fence with barbed wire, white South.
Remember that we're all related, for them and for you.
Invisible common sense, invisible on the census,
invisible murder.

Legislature snickers.
Retract, relax, and pay a tax
I supplant old ideas that are not
serving my highest good
with those that feel good to me.
I trust my intuition.
I trust my Creator.

Unrequited American Lover

Blamed for being black,
a crime against God.
Ask God to testify.
Ask him why.
Fingerprints on cotton,
finger-pointing pricks, fingers pricked
and woven into the seams of this earth.

I was unborn here.
In my belly is the embryo of yellow-eared corn,
blue-eyed scorn, cotton-eared thickets and thorns.
The whole of America is a crime scene,
black DNA on every acre unseen.
Still question my scorn with your sneer?

Implants of hatred as I plant seeds.
I have slaved in these American fields to feed
this country's economic needs,
gave birth to slaves for America's zeal.

Made in Africa, sold for America.
Birthed from Africa, aborted in America.
Stolen from Africa, belabored in America.
I've labored for my entire life,
birthing a future for your entitled wife
as you've sold mine further south for life.
Black's sweat and blood then fertilized these crops.
If I'm caught unconscious, it'll be all for naught.

I envision a world in which people co-exist harmoniously.
It is my birthright to live freely and happily in my skin.
I am unapologetically a beautiful, Black woman.
I am reclaiming my personal power.

Being Black in Public

Mom turned early grave digger.
It's not safe for a nigger.
Good lord, don't let them see me.
They'll see the me they portray on TV
that fits in the cavernous cavity
of their cankerous proclivity.
Good lord, don't let them see me
through the lens of their
handed-down belief systems
Dangle the country-fried carrot
with no relief system
off-white power.
Sudden fascination
with the off-white wall paint,
rather the black wallflower,
colored eyes filled with disdain.
Agitation of logic with that questioning look.
A black reading a book?
Without a spine they try to confine
us to their paperback version of the "excursion".
The hairs on my arm raise

as high as the turned nose.
Good lord, don't let them see me.
The me who's less than
the me they can reprimand, disband,
brand, and can't stand. Not the me that can
withstand, stand, ain't bland,
with the right strand of hair,
of DNA, of blood, of stripes and stars.
Not the me that's stranded here in the
stale energy of American fear.
Gave up the ghost, crippled and bleeding,
by those living on the bright side of the veil.
(Can't figure out why there's a frown
on the fruit of stolen crops, corrupt crowns,
and stolen labor.
Cropped out the black figure,
blacks dismembered,
blacks dissed and stories not remembered.
Black woman in labor with a blue-eyed mixed
... feelings toward the savior.)
The hostility unseen, puss in the public eye
retracting their gaze. Opportunity privatized,
facial features disfigured, displaced with a trigger.
I give myself permission to feel all my emotions.
I hold space for my emotions without judgment.
I release all false programming surrounding my skin color.
I give myself permission to transcend cultural biases.
I find sanctuary within.
I am focused on the one thing which I can control: myself.
I am transcending generational pain

through awareness and inspired action.
I am a conscious creator.

Nesting Dolls

I sit here waiting
like a minimum wage worker
after a long shift.
Unbeknownst to me,
the bus broke down
right along with my mind
on a route to a dead end.
Optimistic in naivety,
sitting here in the problem
waiting for something
to pick me up and move me forward.
Something that will reanimate me,
answer the question of me.
Something I'm still becoming.
That external something which isn't coming.
I am the vehicle.
So I sit like the little girl who sat,
phone receiver heavy in her hand,
hearing the utterances of father's false promises.
Broken before made, sitting in her DNA
an inheritance of ancestral trauma.

She was broken before made
and I sit as heavy as a protestor
whose lungs cough up black smoke,
internally combusting.
Praying for black lives to glass gods in glass skies.
I sit here in between,
swinging my feet from the edge
of another dimension
like the drug-addicted 20-something-year-old
who doesn't know if she's coming down or died again.
And I sit like a nesting doll,
each girl I've been within me,
praying that my feet,
heavy from carrying them all,
move us forward.
Like a cinder block waiting for the wind,
like time would reciprocate the gesture,
as if I were the no one that time waits for.
I am healing all past versions of myself.
I am sending love to myself at all developmental stages.
I am worthy.
I always have been.
I always will be.
I am royalty.

I Am a Woman of Grace and Dignity (At least that's what my sponsor thinks)

Provoked in Thought

A life of lies, bitterness, sadness,
anger, hatred, and hurt.
My therapist posed a simple question
that waged a war between denial and delusion:
When did this downward spiral start?
Like glaciers rapidly shifting apart.
The demolition of an omnipresent idol,
a statue that I devoutly worshipped and glorified.
Placed faith in a feigned father:
Stev... Rather, Inmate of a Correctional Facility—
that's far more fitting.
One question
capable of simultaneously placing
an insurmountable amount of pressure on my throat
and an inescapable heaviness on my heart.
Choking on the reality of my childhood.
A truth that ruptured innocence,
cold enlightenment at which I still wince—
outer skin withering away in a river

of spit spewed from the mouths
of my inner demons,
existing in their physical form:
my mother and father.
Self-worth which they desecrated,
modeling violence and an assorted tin of abuse,
unworthy pretenders which He delegated.
Of the darkness
a deeper ask
a deeper answer
Alchemists, we are the transmutation
the transformation through affirmation
I am recognized for my excellence.
I am recognized for my unique attributes.
I have a healthy sense of self-esteem.
I am celebrated.
People love me.
It's my time.
I deserve to have it all.

The Hoarder

A dreamer in a wasteland.
A maggot in sand,
crowded with cardboard minds,
hoarding words to remember mine
hoarding truth that I seldom find.
I express as my authentic self.
I am choosing the beliefs that best serve me.
I am weird and weird is wonderful.
I am weird and wonderful.
I love my writing.
My books sell out within hours of being released.
My books are collector items.
I make wise decisions.
I am a dreamer with a plan of action.
I am consciously creating my reality.

The Psychic Reader

Darkened eyes plastered
beneath white walls.
I can feel the air watching me,
black face, devil between blue lips.
I can feel them trying to walk inside my body,
child's voice in the background.
I can hear them trying to influence me.
I stay above as they stay low.
I choose light.
I am light.
I am trusting myself.

Unsalable

Splinters from the wood of Jesus's cross
in my crossed fingers.
Cross a prayer task off the list
of the ego-driven blasphemous
ass who harasses Mary's ashes i
n the casket at mass where the mass-murdering
deity tells me with gaiety
he sees the light in me,
and I see that he's full flight
from my reality.
False humility, falsifying empathy
to connect with me, silly me.
Convection oven burns me to a different degree,
and I put my hand on it again
thinking it'll happen differently.
That's the insanity.
String you along by the hair of your pride,
by the skin of your stride.
False humility, lost the human in me,
connecting robotically.
Forced connection, force that is myself

forced to reckon with, reckon
I'm equipped to let my lips overload
my tact as I stab God in the back.
Take my will back and again I black out,
filled with demons and doubt and still false humility.
False positive on a false test for false admission
into the gates of heaven. I'm superior,
for you all are God's chores.
I chortle at the core.
Two-faced faces facing opposite directions,
half-shuffled church of cards.
Fallen angels have no regard
for the halfway house superstars.
I am but a vessel.
I am one of millions of messengers.
I am a clear channel.
I am offering myself to God.
I am a servant, not servile.

Telekinesis

If I think about what you think about me enough,
I can predict the worst thing you might think about me,
and then think about how I can navigate my way through
that situation so that the very small part of my self-esteem
remains intact and doesn't suffer too hard from me falling
on the face that I've shown you.

I am in love with who I am.
I am confident.
I am free to express in ways that feel genuine to me.
I am allowing my emancipation from expectation.
I am easy on myself today.

Trauma

Trauma answers to the call of my name in my voice,
responds with my body.
Thievery of presence in broad daylight,
glowering at spectators with brazen cocksureness,
it seizes my charm, confidence, and calm.
Once burning with desire, now lukewarm intentions
block connection like a brain clot.
At potential threats neurons will fire.
Saber tooth tigers and wolves live
in the periphery of my mind:
in every social situation, in every conversation.
I am a conscious creator.
I am compassionate.
I am complete.
I am whole.
I am consistent.
I am disciplined.
I am prayerful.
I am useful.
I am talented.

The Myth of Madness

Trying on each psychological disorder
for size, each genetic jinx.
Pattern, perpetuation, and panic,
the cause to have cursed my lineage.
Label me something
that comes with a prescription bottle,
that makes me feel something
so that it's no longer bottled up.
Diagnosed sane with live-in pain.
It was inherited in childhood
from a father that was
self-absorbed, sex addicted, and self-drugged
from a mother he couldn't love,
so anguish grew in darkness
beneath her eyes. It festered deep inside
her posture, weakened her stride.
Poor self-worth lives deep inside
of pockets in her spine.
Dragging her leg behind her,
dragging his tail behind him,
dragging their offspring behind them,

too heavy to carry on.
The buzzing of flies sounds different
when it's your baby's future they're feasting on.
Ancestral pain unresolved
won't be willed away with wishing.
Transgenerational transmission
of the enormity of unresolved obscenities
that have welled up for centuries,
energetically imprinted on my DNA.
Pain that I am privy to transcend
now that the demons are at bay.
Will someone please give me permission
to remain this way?
I am here.
I deserve to be here in this world.
I have arrived with a purpose.
I raise the frequency of the energy in the space that I occupy.
I am healing my lineage through conscious choices.

Anxiety

It's the feeling you get
right after you decide against
speaking the words that have long ago
grown into mildew coating the surface of your tongue,
right as the esophagus has swollen to such an extent
that air can no longer nurture
your quickly shriveling lungs,
and when the bone structure of your jaw turns to dust
from being out of use for so long.
It's the feeling you get as tightly clenched teeth
prevent the most inaudible of sighs from being heard.
And even though an upright posture is preferred,
the body contracts into the fetal position,
mimicking the heart's vulnerability.
Womb is to pericardium: emotional infertility.

I am present.
I am okay.
I am trusting in the Spirit of this Universe.
I am trusting in the process.
I am safe.

I am safe.
I am safe.
I am fabulous and fulfilled.

Know-It-All

I've gotta talk about every topic
that life has ever made me an expert on
because if I don't,
then people will think
that I'm not smart
and that's all I've got: brains for beauty,
and my self-esteem is so deeply intertwined
in the standing ovation,
and everyone has to love me
or I'm not good enough
and my veins crave validation.
Because I've never been good at gray,
just feeling gray, but not feeling while in the gray,
just filling in the gray with pinks,
like rose and fuchsia, or black.
Tinted lenses, rose colored shades or blackened fuchsia.
I am still.
I am connected to Infinite Intelligence.
I am beautiful.
I am trusting my inner knowing.

Crazy Glue

How can I think about how my mind
does or doesn't work with my own mind
—a mind that thinks about itself.
A mind that eats itself.
Picking the skin off of the bone.
I thought it wasn't obvious
where the cracks were,
but the crazy glue still shows
and I'm embarrassed that all along
people have known, except for me.
I am practicing self-care.
I am taking care of my mental health.
I am separate from my mind.
I am using more and more of my mind intentionally.

I Worked at a Car Dealership

The automobile industry
in *auto*pilot and im*mobilized in dust.*
A habit that has inhabited and inhibited
ambition, an automaton in an intimate
relationship with a screen, screening for
a connection while streaming reality.
Worth determined by performance,
each platform a forum for forging
a partnership plutonic in nature,
malformed by egocentric and economic erasure.
There's an album in my albumen.
Ate when the 8-track was played back,
pro-teen abortion and sound absorption.
Algorithm of a sick system,
another Valium for the volume.
Venus met with vehemence of the behemoths.
Pinned amongst the pinstripes
of suits and starless-eyed,
needle-nosed opinions of salesmen,

I wear a talisman to throw off the tallest of them.
Performing so well
that now my wrists are deformed and swell.
Email after email pitching promotion after sale,
approved credit and qualifications.
Dedication becomes self-deprecation,
each screen a scrying mirror,
a portal that prostitutes productivity.
I make phone calls for a living.
Phone rings in the key of E.
Prospecting for new unsuspecting buyers
without a backbone or a bias,
punching my card in a time loop:
Ctrl-C Ctrl-P Ctrl-Alt-Delete Me Ctrl-d Me.
My paintings hang in museums around the world.
I am advancing every day.
I am becoming more and more famous every day.
My art is becoming more and more masterly every day.
My relationship with my art is always deepening.
My art and poetry are progressing.
I am getting smarter and wealthier by the minute.
It is easy for me to think positively.
It is easy for me to expound upon positive thoughts.
It is easy for me to be happy.
I am getting wealthier by the second.
I am progressing every day.
It is easy for me to love myself.
I am a best-selling author, motivational speaker,
and famous artist.
I am well studied.

I capture the essence of my subject in portraits.
I pour my heart into all that I create.
The image is impressed upon my mind's eye
before I receive the commission.
The right ideas always come to mind.
I always know the perfect way to express an idea or emotion.
I have added a lot of beauty and good into this world.
I am the published author of many books.

Poetry Submission

So what
if it doesn't fit
as tight as the skin of your predilection
and stingy rules in your gentrified genre of genius?
And so what if the rhymes are as off as I am my rocker,
format malformed like my genetic marker?
Neither my poetry nor I will submit,
grammar gone off the deep end of the margin,
and I into the belly of boundless blue lines.
I peer through the small holes
which are secret portals into imagination.
Fulfillment that's deeper than the warmth of
December's expectations,
false humility, fenced humanity.
The postponement of empathy until
forced affinity, crippling insanity
for the consequence is befriended.
Forged prosperity, inorganic so not sustained.

I don't deserve the praise
the alcoholic prays.

On yesterday's laurels
he stays and fades,
morally more or less unchanged,
merrily score suppress the pain.
Emotionally sore
he lives in shame

Knucklehead virgin knees
mercifully more confessed and changed,
compliments killin' me.
What more can he store within his veins?
Confidence sickening.
Mercifully pour, confess the shame.
Fastest affinity. False humility, dead-ended ability.
He washed up ashore on misery lane.
Address or dress the shame,
confess or regress the same.
Profess and undress the claim,
digest the maimed.
A crutch that impedes.
Dark spirits stampede,
phantom foot spasm of glamor and greed.
Repent behaviors that I repeat.
Left Midas at the crack house
in exchange for instant pain relief,
alchemy not quick enough for me.
Heart of Midas fashioned in fool's gold,
forging a crown into a crack pipe.
Taped shoe soles soul sold
fool's goals turned scripture into a script.

Thought teeter tottering at the tip of the tongue,
talking in troubled tongues
washed out with serpents at a forked road.
What am I?
My writing blesses, heals, and inspires people.
The perfect words
always come to me, and I will
know that they are coming
from you, Source Energy.
I trust that I will always receive them.
I will always allow them to come.
My voice will elevate others.
My words will transmute darker energies.
My words create harmony for others.
I have a healing tongue.
I always know what to say.
My voice will elevate others.
The sound of my voice is healing.
I use my voice to empower others.
I speak to free people.
I speak to with the intention to create good in life,
and so it is.
And so it is done. Thank you.
I am a creator.
I am energy.
I am elevated.
I am gold.

The Writer

Words arranged like funerary flowers,
an offering to faeries.
Juxtaposed emotion and time
exploring the unknown mind unspoken, divine.
Who caged the writer?
Who clipped my wings?
Who gouged out my tongue?
Mirrored reflection stares pointedly at me.
Untaught, so forbidden?
Genetic genius to remain hidden?
To the naysayers in my head, good riddance.
If I give this all of me,
all that I've got sourced from within myself,
it will be but a return to self,
for this is who I am.
A writer, that I am born to be.
If I allow the conjured creativity
to possess my art,
if I hold an electric eagerness
in the furrow of my brow,
if I stare off into space

in surety and contemplation,
if I allow the right words
to impregnate my mental womb,
if I draw upon the energy
of words and swords and wounds and sounds
from the collective unconscious,
if I allow each draft of self to express through the craft,
if I allow each verse of each version to vindicate my voice
in faith of the stream of articulation and inspiration t
hat is infinite,
if I mime the memories and moments of the masses,
if I allow the stress of each syllable to alleviate my own,
if I can purge pain into poetry or prose,
the pages will be written of a purpose fulfilled
and a dream enclosed.
I am sharing my gifts with the world.
I am.
I am a lighthouse and a powerhouse.
I am here to raise my frequency.
I am here to do this by aligning with source.
I am here to do this by creating.
I am here to do this by remaining open to love.
I am here to do this through love.
I am here to love others.
I am guided by the Divine Mother.

Pockets

Tourmaline and garlic cloves in my pocket
crowded with singed sage leaves.
Smugly, I thought the smudge stick
would remain whole this time
like my spiritual condition in a marriage so astringent
when layers are peeled back.
Scorching the salivating tongue
of the conditioned wife who keeps drinking
water to put out the fire
caused by years
of swallowing too much alcohol
and inhaling the sage smoke.
It may have been enough if the leaves weren't crushed
like our hearts from trying,
if the resin bore a resolution
and the smudge didn't stick,
but there's not enough room left
in my pocket for any more pride,
so I begin to breathe fire too
and the palace in the clouds bursts into flames.
I am respected.

I am respected.
I am respected.
I am respecting myself.
I am respecting myself even when
it's not the easiest.
I am creating and keeping healthy boundaries.
I am protecting my energy.
I am sacred.
I am sacred.
I am sacred.

I Must Be Rid

Skin sunken into bones,
body heavy with anxiety,
esophageal Charley horse.
I must be rid of anxiety
or remain emotionally quarantined,
socially maladjusted, rusted self-esteem.
The cruelty of sweat against white linen,
stoic pretense dampened, stifling all beginnings.
Thick, dense, hot and hard air between us
that slows thought, that captures thought
in a net of self-ridicule.

Betrayal is the peculiar face twitch
heaving with limitations.
My hand swats at the desperation in my joints
as my blood becomes too heavy for my body.
I must be rid of anxiety.

I am becoming increasingly aware
of how my thinking influences my actions.
I am comfortable with who I am.

I am confident.
I am unconcerned with other people's perceptions.
I am not less than or better than anyone else.
I am intrinsically deserving.
I am making a conscious decision to love myself.
I am aware of the value of my emotions.
I am grateful for the state of awareness
from which I can then make a change.

Social MEDIA-crity

Fixated on a potential version
that lives in a possible future
misaligned with current actions
like mechanical smile and motive.
Image yearned, not earned,
a dream in an urn outside of time.
A decision dead on the line,
a spool of stagnation,
a person undone could have become,
but ashamed of the valleys
pulled in by the mouth of the mountain,
audaciousness of your inauthenticity.
Be real,
your pain is
pixelated still.
Social mediocrity filtered into the gray area
of a scaled back self-acceptance.
Cease with sizing up scars,
fuck the comparisons.
Love yourself,
pledge allegiance to you,

question the societal inheritance
of beliefs that serve who?
I am releasing all judgment.
I am comparing myself to only my past self.
I am grounded in that which is real.

Woman

It was so important that I be *heard*
that I raised my voice
and lowered my standards.
The mental shrapnel that deepens the scandal,
the emotional self of which I've lost a handle.
Raised my voice and lowered my standards.
Lifted my dress and laid on my back.
Straightened my hair and painted my face.
Lowered my pride and raised my brow.
In an iris colored with perversion,
in the reflection of a funhouse mirror version—
Is it possible to lose a self, yet to be found?
I love the journey that my soul has chosen.
I am in love with the person I am.
I accept myself as the woman that I am.
I made a conscious decision to incarnate as a woman.
I am enjoying healthy sexual relations.
I am present and vulnerable.
I am worthy of giving and receiving pleasure.
I enjoy exploratory sex.

I love the body that I am in.
I approve of myself.
I am enough.
I am releasing all codependent pitfalls and programming.

Transactional
Worshipper

I'm a transactional worshipper
worshipping that which worships me
in dividends, and I'm invested if I win.
Not working with a full deck, my girlfriend said to me.
The last card in my half deck
a lowercase ace lowering myself.
The odour of societal distaste
busies the air outside of my body.
Inside the church of cards
half shuffled with grace
the dealer's face as ambiguous as my faith
inside the house of God, halfway house of cards.
Praise dancing in combat boots and lingerie.
Prayers to self for daily breadcrumbs.
Gluten free, guiltless, materialistic gluttony.
Blessings stained with religious debt
half-heartedly cut with regret.

My dear,
in this sphere of glassy-eyed cheers
quarreling with once acquainted queers,
and yearning for yesteryears
in this strange nest of bedazzled bedevilments,
of stale beers and soulless sex
in this realm of rooms, of bar stools and broken rules,
of blood orange oval-shaped regrets,
scarlet sheets scorched from cigarettes,
mosaic shards and cracked chandeliers,
in bathroom stalls where dreams are fears,
where how much cocaine in a line meant
how far out of alignment I'd get.
This is where we found it,
and where I lost myself
and who you thought I was.

Thin lines
between lifelines,
red lines,
razor blades,
fat white lines
flat line,
deadline.

Identity Crisis

An androgynous deity,
sexual disorientation disguised,
dressed in a woman's body,
baffled by my own biology.
At eighteen, I disclosed to my mother
that I fancied women.
With a smile that bore discreet dismay,
she said, I've always known, and I'll always love you.
But the rest of my family certainly didn't.
I was the apple that fell far from the fucking tree,
rolled down a slope into a hole where the watermelons
grow, rotted, and was then cross pollinated
with an extinct flower.

My mother lied, anyway.

I am allowed to love whoever I want.
I am allowed to be whoever I want.
To love and be loved are my divine birthrights.
I am the rainbow.

The Pariah & the Piranha

Romance riddled with curiosity
of unexamined potential:
pariah partnered with a piranha.
I continue to pray
as she continues to prey
on my prana,
unconscious in her actions,
haphazardly flailing negative seeds
that breathe and breed mental disease
in the troubled water of our shared mind.

She chose self-bondage
rather than to rummage
through her subconscious rubbish
and cultivate a higher version of herself.
With greater self awareness,
higher moral standards,
another inch of empathy,
compassion in place of chaos,
patience instead of panic,
emotional intelligence,

in lieu of irreverence—
Her singsong voice:
I'm using you, amusing you, a muse in you abused too.
I replied:
I'm used to you, used to abuse, used up and useless, too.

I am a lover.
I am emotionally intelligent.
I choose to forgive.
I choose to forgive.
I choose to forgive.
I am putting myself first today.

Feline Frequency

It's the catcall of the straight man to the lesbian
whom he has identified as gender conforming
to the rise in his pants.
The fall of her faith
speaking directly to her trauma,
bypassing conscious mind and comma.
Unsolicited, not unwanted pain,
body shudders in twisted pleasure.
Past hurt pounces upon present resolutions to heal.
A sickened thrill travels up the spine,
attention is savored beneath the tongue,
hidden from the palate, but distaste still dissolves.
A part of her enjoys tempting his power,
even if it means relinquishing her personal power,
and this sordid exchange as she walks by, being devoured,
waiting for someone else's eyes to tell her what she's worth.
Violation has a vice grip on validation,
and the length of his wind blows up her skirt.

I am worthy.
I am worth more than my body.

Self-Departed

Witching well wishing unwell.
Between her legs, my tail.
Relationship failed.
I don't need you, but pardon me,
a part in me that hasn't departed me
still wants to feed you.
I need you but you left me,
allegedly pardoning me from your insanity
is what you said to me, and you believed you.
I relied on what I knew: that I wasn't good enough for you,
so you'd found someone new.
I don't need you,
and when apart from me,
don't start with me.
You feed, too, on God or who?
I follow the trail of mixed emotions,
pheromones drenched in compulsion.
You picked up on the scent of my devotion.
I was licked by your liquid potion,
codependent convulsions.
You left with what was left

of what was once me at my best,
left with a regressed and undressed shadow self, unless . . .
I'll place on the top shelf a new sense of self,
a sober version on the verge of emerging
as my authentic self.
Too weak to reach the top shelf.
Gave you my personal power and left myself bereft.
Shelves of selves assailed the selves.
Shelves of selves,
shelves of dead skin cells,
prisoners of selves.
As important to you as a single cell
in a self-made cell, trying to sell myself to you.
To sail higher, I used to use you to use me, never free.
Bottom feed on debris.
To any degree
I'd wait and wait,
and wade and wade,
and waste away for you.
I was never waiting for you in particular,
as long as it was someone— even if that someone,
that somebody was just a corpse, just a body
filled with life
or filled with dread,
filled with fillers instead
that loiter in my head,
that litter what's unsaid,
that lie with us in bed.
In some ways we are all living,
and we're all fucking dead.

We all want to be fucked
to not feel dead,
so I used it and bruised it.
Bruised your body, used your body
as a surrogate for my mother, for my father,
for my lover, for my altar.
Bruised my ego like uncoagulated thought.
Satan's sanctuary I sought.
You used my ego against me
in this emotional onslaught
as my ego would conspire
against me, with you, against me.
Stomp on the seeds of my desires.
She's a black crow born from the fire.
Forego need. Hold me,
that me of which was made a mockery.
You must have cataracts on your pineal gland.
I can't withstand and I can't stand you
when you've left you, and you've left me, too.
You stand for the farmed sheep,
who stare at the crows, scared to croak or make a peep.
You are the voice of the sheep
who surrendered their tonsils for slaughter.
Little Bo Peep. Little woes,
little weeping willow,
weep your woes unto this pillow and sleep.
Advocating for the blind swine doesn't make you brave.
It makes you a slave,
and I'm a shadow on the wall of a cave
in your cardiac chamber that's concave.

I am content with my own company.

Lost My Voice Again

To blame you is easier
So
You hid it from me!
pressed into the ridges of your soul
like human shit in humidity
of sweltering pride,
like stale gum stuck
with primordial spit
trailing tears where my tubes untied,
watched my shadow split
like jailhouse cum.
The noise of your negativity
like razor blades over skin cells
crushed me creatively
like crayon beneath fingernails
I hid it from you in compassion,
where you'd never look.
I am protecting the gifts God gave me.

Relapse

The end relapsed, veiled memories
pale and borrowed from an etheric lapse.
Seemingly eternal eclipse.
A walk-in, a night out. A side of myself
I've never seen pulled something within that has no skin.
As the room began to snicker, I was giving in,
the influence darkened.
Solution in quicksand in my glass house.
Rock bottoms and glass basements,
broken bones and black outs,
brown paper bags and broken homes.
An honorary nose upturned.
I can outsmart this cunning foe.
Palms blistered and stretching,
life line unsewn,
clinging onto the calamity.
Clutching a will not meant for my hold.
"Quit Playing God,"
only then will the miracles unfold.
The nervousness and heart palpitations,
yesterday's alcohol digesting my perception of now.

The self-piteous plight and plea to be free.
The casting downward of an incessantly pounding head.
Will I ever be back in my right mind again?
Lord, take the taste away from me. Will I ever stay sober?
I am sober.
I love myself.
I honor my spirit.
I am on the right path.
I make healthy decisions.
I am becoming the best version of myself.
Gratitude for my sobriety:
I am grateful that I make the next right,
not next available, decision.
I am grateful for a constantly evolving
relationship with my Creator.
I am grateful for an opportunity
to turn my pain into my purpose,
madness into magic, and misery into ministry.
I am grateful for the opportunity to serve others.

51st Street

Call an ambulance! I screamed.
You won't be needing that, my mother replied.
We both gawked at her
unmoving
form
13 stories below.
51 threads of self unspooled,
51 spools of fool,
51 spun out in dread,
51 hung out and dead.
If I knew the trees would catch me, I would fall.
The sky fell from her eyes
and of a body she was absolved.
Uphill battles, downward spirals.
An Achilles hell down in the bayou.
Down in the bayou up shit's creek,
offering lies to false idols.
False heartbeat.
Head murmur.
Down in the bayou.
I am accepting uncertainty.

I am releasing all control.

They Told Me You Weren't Dead

They told me that you still live
without form,
beyond sensory perception
on the outliers of logic,
in an overlap,
a quantum gap
outside of space
occupying different dimensions
simultaneously in consciousness.
For the first time,
I have peace of mind
that our love transcends
any construct of time.
I am that which is timeless

A dormant Depression

Midsection misshapen with excess skin,
circumstance that self-hatred fed,
acting behind closed curtains.
My funeral to be held in your head.
Fickle situations, transient relationships.
Fleeting lovers, different jobs,
changing roles: states, statues, hearts, and hues.
My most rehearsed, least confessed
discursive thoughts a puppeteer to happiness.
This old familiar sorrow once departed,
twice returned, a dependency on impending doom.
I am moving forward.
My personal values and views are more important than society's.

Rendezvous with a Mute Narcissist

Coming home to erasure,
looking for closure
in the closet once full of possessions,
now emptied of expression.
Diminishing return,
lesson earned.
It's hearsay until I hear you say that you won't stay,
but there's this delay.
This pause is purgatory,
has weakened my pride.
It only grows when hidden inside.
My ego can't share the humor.
On my hubris there's a tumor.
Thought you could embalm me with lies
while you were spreading your thighs.
You know I'm hurting, yet you're still deserting.
Traces of you.
These faces are new.
Oh, how did I misconstrue

the gibberish you knew to spew?
You never put me first.
You continued to rehearse
lines of our love in reverse.
We lived in your house of mirrors
where you'd saunter around in your pageant gown.
I am focusing on my relationship with God.
I am faith focused.
I am welcoming the right person.

Cracks in the Marble

There are cracks in the marble.
Demolition of the matriarchal,
structure of a broken hierarchical system.
Cyst on stem cells of the culture
feasting on the fetus like a vulture,
an inheritance of torture.
Your obstructed vision corrupted my peace.
Your lymph nodes erupted
and minimized my grief
which grew into a grudge.
Your optic nerve has interrupted
your right thinking,
sending smoke signals to your left brain,
unchanged and unblinking.
You change, I relive the same pain.
I change unashamed, you stay the same.
Cracks in the marble,
fall of the matriarchal
reign.
Waded in your emotional over pour,
railroaded into your darkness,

fought your demons as you created more.
There are cracks in the marble,
demolition of the matriarchal.
Porcelain face such a waste,
lured in by the size of your fickle promise.
Now just trying to erase traces of you,
every facet, perspective askew.
You held no space for me,
I held space for two.
You felt displaced with me.
Well, she can't love me no more,
covered in bed sores as a fuss is made of folklore.
Love for self an optical illusion,
eyes sunken in and bruising.
Bad blood coursing,
emotional transfusion.
Days spent in a dream and a drunken delusion,
self-indulgent in self-seclusion,
my importance to you drawn to a conclusion.
We help one another gracefully
move back toward consciousness.
We honor and love one another's inner child.
We respect one another

Layaway Lovers

Monetized Monogamy
A lover placed on layaway
found between the cushions.
Vibrational currency scraped up
with the same frantic nature
that the guilty collect themselves with
when caught in the wrong decision and wrong bed.
Placeholder in a shadow
worn into a formless friendship.
It's already been lived.
Our honeymoon high- and low-end.
A winged frame like hers taunts the hermit,
exploits his insecurity.
Self-esteem fashioned of day drinks,
a mind which liquifies
when the other head on his shoulders disappears.
The two of us and our drugs wanting love.
Companion plant to a rose.
Our tasteless, insoluble reality
with an almost-aliveness
that intimidates the weary

like a clock with only a long hand.
Failing flowers.
Money see evil
and how it obliterates,
monkey do evil and often it liberates.
In ruins reminiscing over a runaway romance, '
I took my lover off layaway.
We help one another suffer less.
We are energetically there for one another.

The Actress

Why do I give you such important lines in the play?
I cast you— for Christmas, my birthday, for every day.
Why do I dim my spotlight for you?
Casting my pearl to such swine
when anyway, you'll improvise,
intentions fluorescent rouge.
Behind the scenes: blow out my candles,
breath of your wailing, waxen wishes.
I to scrub the glasses
stained with anger, washed of your sin.
Next year,
outgrow this selfish skin.
My spiritual partner and I share in sacred intimacy.
We share in a special closeness.
We function as one.
We co-exist on the same frequencies.
We make decisions with one another's best interests in mind.
We make actions toward one another with love and intention.
We treat each other with tenderness and care.
We are supportive of one another's goals and dreams.
We are attuned to one another and know when

and what the other person needs emotionally.